Dedication

To my family for all the years of celebrating the Christmas story together.
To my husband, Gene, who encourages, consults, and supports all my efforts.

This Presented with Joy to

Joy in the Midst Publishing 2023
Story and Pictures Copyright © 2023
All rights reserved.

THE HOLY BIBLE, NEW INTERNATIONAL VERSION®, NIV®
Copyright © 1973, 1978, 1984, 2011 by Biblica, Inc.®
Used by permission. All rights reserved worldwide.

Tips for Celebrating with "O Glorious Hope"

*Vary reading and singing to suit your family dynamics.
*Wee Ones: Words float on the page. Be sure to point, clap, make hand motions to encourage your wee one to participate.
*Primary Ages: The Christmas story is paraphrased for young children on picture pages. Feel free to skip the full scriptures until your children are older.
*Ages 9-90: Full scriptures are included on separate pages. Add these as children grow.
*Songs: The first verse of hymns are located in a box shape. Sing along even if you have a terrible voice. God enjoys the joyful noise.
*Create a family tradition, read the story every year on Christmas Eve or Morning.

Worship and Enjoy

O Glorious Hope

Now in the sixth month the angel Gabriel was sent by God to a city of Galilee named Nazareth, to a virgin betrothed to a man whose name was Joseph, of the house of David. The virgin's name was Mary. And having come in, the angel said to her, Rejoice, highly favored one, the Lord is with you; blessed are you among women!" (Luke 1: 26-28)

"Do not be afraid, Mary, for you have found favor with God. And behold, you will conceive in your womb and bring forth a Son, and shall call His name Jesus. He will be great, and will be called the Son of the Highest; and the Lord God will give Him the throne of His father David. And He will reign over the house of Jacob forever, and of His kingdom there will be no end." (Luke 1:30-33)

And Mary said, "My soul magnifies the Lord and my spirit rejoices in God my Savior. (Luke 1: 46-47)

And it came to pass in those days that a decree went out
from Caesar Augustus that all the world should be registered.
This census first took place while Quirinius was governing Syria.
So all went to be registered, everyone to his own city.

Joseph also went up from Galilee, out of the city of Nazareth,
into Judea, to the city of David, which is called Bethlehem,
because he was of the house and lineage of David,
to be registered with Mary, his betrothed wife,
who was with child.

(Luke 2: 1-5)

Some two thousand years ago, God sent his son, Jesus, to earth. This is the true story of the birth of Jesus and His amazing love.

O Holy Night, the stars are brightly shining. It is the night of our dear Saviors birth.

So it was, that while they were there, the days were completed for her to be delivered. And she brought forth her firstborn Son, and wrapped Him in swaddling cloths, and laid Him in a manger, because there was no room for them in the inn. (Luke 2: 6-7)

Find the stable

O little town of Bethlehem
How still we see thee lie
Above thy deep and dreamless sleep
The silent stars go by.
Yet in the dark street shineth
The everlasting light
The hopes and fears of all the years
Are met in thee tonight.

The city was crowded. The inn was full. So Mary and Joseph had to stay in a stable with the animals.

Now there were in the same country shepherds living out in the fields, keeping watch over their flock by night. And behold, an angel of the Lord stood before them, and the glory of the Lord shone around them, and they were greatly afraid.

Then the angel said to them, "Do not be afraid, for behold, I bring you good tidings of great joy which will be to all people. For there is born to you this day in the city of David a Savior, who is Christ the Lord. And this will be the sign to you: You will find a Babe wrapped in swaddling cloths, lying in a manger.

"And suddenly there was with the angel a multitude of the heavenly host praising God and saying, "Glory to God in the highest, And on earth peace, goodwill toward men!"
(Luke 2: 8-14)

Wave to the angels

Angels told the shepherds to go see the baby who is Christ the Lord lying in a manger.

So it was, when the angels had gone away from them into heaven, that the shepherds said to one another, "Let us now go to Bethlehem and see this thing that has come to pass, which the Lord has made known to us."

And they came with haste and found Mary and Joseph, and the Babe lying in a manger. Now when they had seen Him, they made widely known the saying which was told them concerning this Child.

And all those who heard it marveled at those things which were told them by the shepherds.
(Luke 2: 15-18)

The heavens declare the glory of God. (Psalm 19:1)
Sing to the Lord, all the earth. Sing to the Lord, bless His name. (Psalm 96:1-2)

Instructions for the next page:
Choose which animal YOU want to be.
Help the animals sing "Hallelujah".

Hallelujah

Hallelujah! Hallelujah!
Hallelujah! Hallelujah!
Hallelujah! Hallelujah!
Hallelujah! Hallelujah!
Hallelujah! Hallelujah!
For ever and ever,
Hallelujah! Hallelujah! Amen.

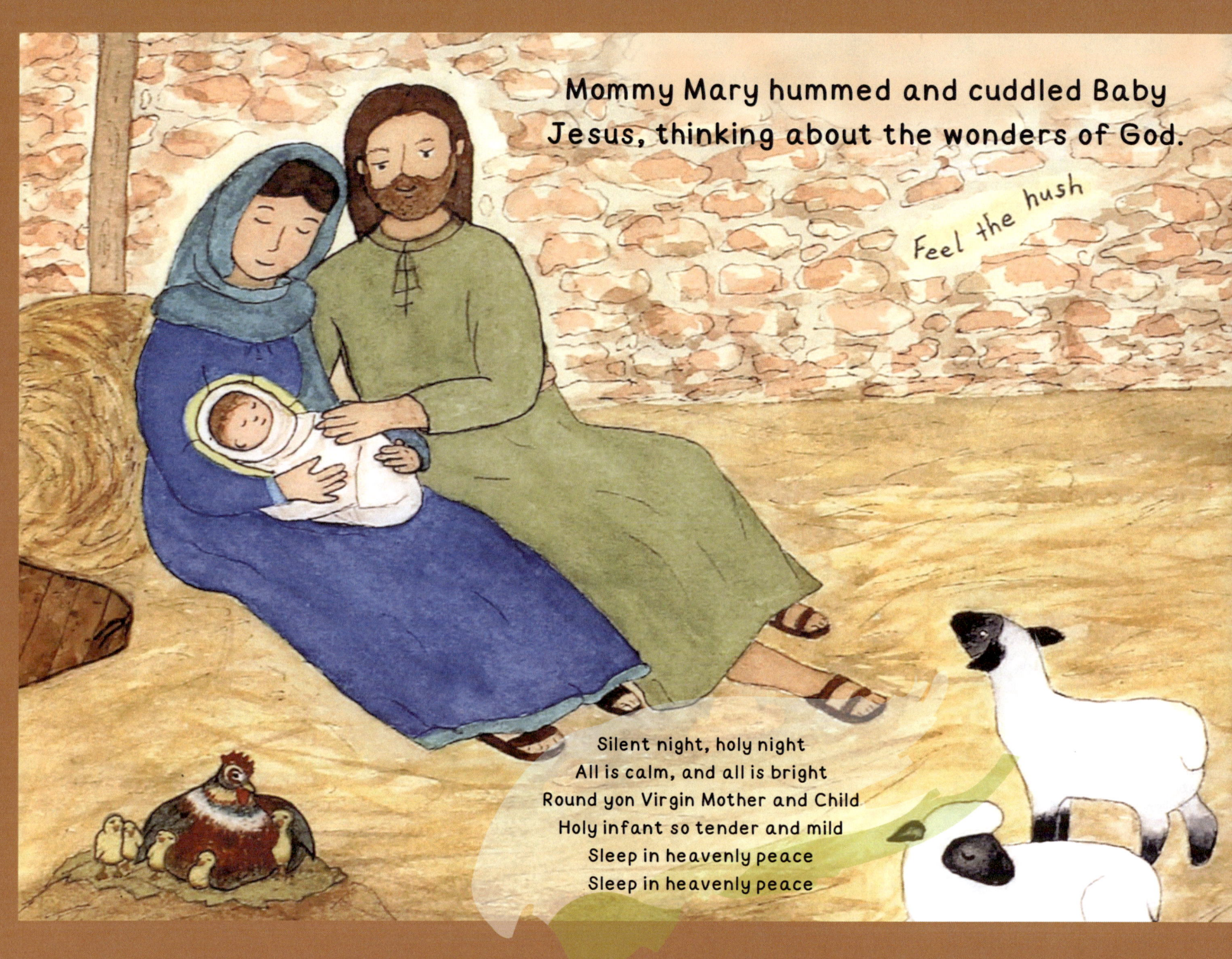

Now after Jesus was born in Bethlehem of Judea in the days of Herod the king, behold, wise men from the East came to Jerusalem, saying, "Where is He who has been born King of the Jews? For we have seen His star in the East and have come to worship Him."

When Herod the king heard this, he was troubled, and all Jerusalem with him. And when he had gathered all the chief priests and scribes of the people together, he inquired of them where the Christ was to be born. So they said to him, "In Bethlehem of Judea, for thus it is written by the prophet:

'But you, Bethlehem, in the land of Judah,
Are not the least among the rulers of Judah;
For out of you shall come a Ruler
Who will shepherd My people Israel.' "

Then Herod, when he had secretly called the wise men, determined from them what time the star appeared. And he sent them to Bethlehem and said, "Go and search carefully for the young Child, and when you have found Him, bring back word to me, that I may come and worship Him also." When they heard the king, they departed; and behold, the star which they had seen in the East went before them, till it came and stood over where the young Child was. (Matthew 2: 2-9)

When they saw the star, they rejoiced with exceedingly great joy.

And when they had come into the house, they saw the young Child with Mary His mother, and fell down and worshiped Him. And when they had opened their treasures, they presented gifts to Him: gold, frankincense, and myrrh.

Then, being divinely warned in a dream that they should not return to Herod, they departed for their own country another way. (Matthew 2: 10-12)

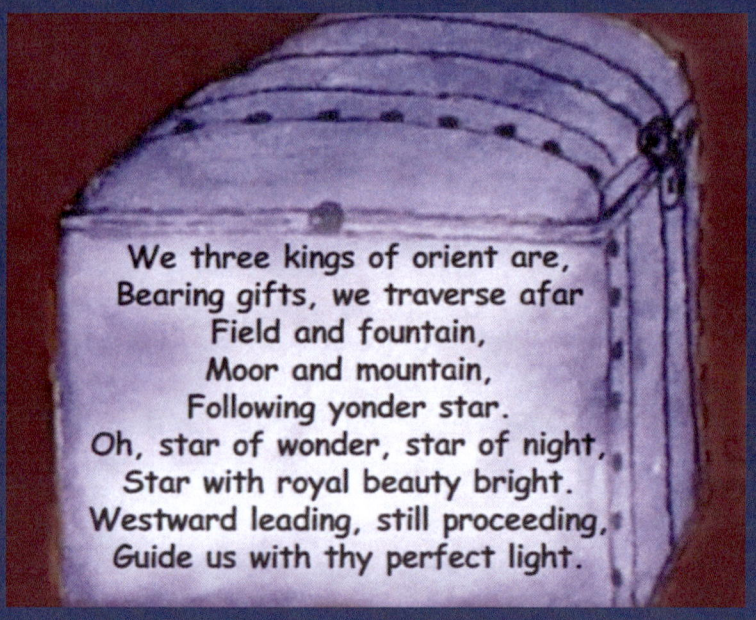

We three kings of orient are,
Bearing gifts, we traverse afar
Field and fountain,
Moor and mountain,
Following yonder star.
Oh, star of wonder, star of night,
Star with royal beauty bright.
Westward leading, still proceeding,
Guide us with thy perfect light.

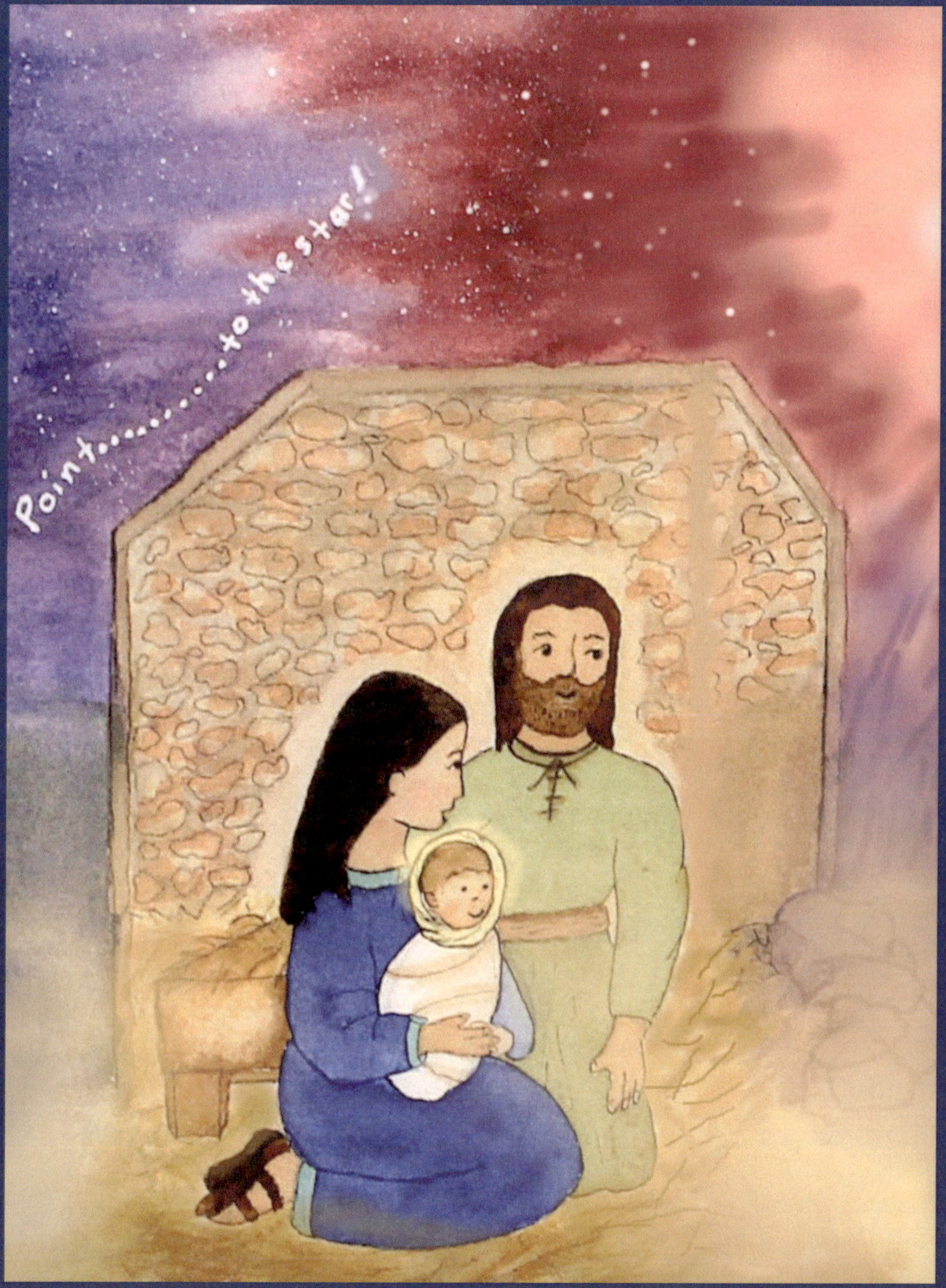
Point..........to the star!

But the Story did not end there...

And the Child grew and became strong in spirit, filled with wisdom; and the grace of God was upon Him. (Luke 2: 40)

His parents went to Jerusalem every year at the Feast of the Passover. And when He was twelve years old, they went up to Jerusalem according to the custom of the feast. When they had finished the days, as they returned, the Boy Jesus lingered behind in Jerusalem. And Joseph and His mother did not know it; but supposing Him to have been in the company, they went a day's journey, and sought Him among their relatives and acquaintances. So when they did not find Him, they returned to Jerusalem, seeking Him.

So it was that after three days they found Him in the temple, sitting in the midst of the teachers, both listening to them and asking them questions. And all who heard Him were astonished at His understanding and answers. So when they saw Him, they were amazed; and His mother said to Him, "Son, why have You done this to us? Look, Your father and I have sought You anxiously."

And He said to them, "Why did you seek Me? Did you not know that I must be about My Father's business?" (Luke 2: 41-49)

Then little children were brought to Him that He might put His hands on them and pray, but the disciples rebuked them. But Jesus said, "Let the little children come to Me, and do not forbid them; for of such is the kingdom of heaven."
(Matthew 19: 13-14)

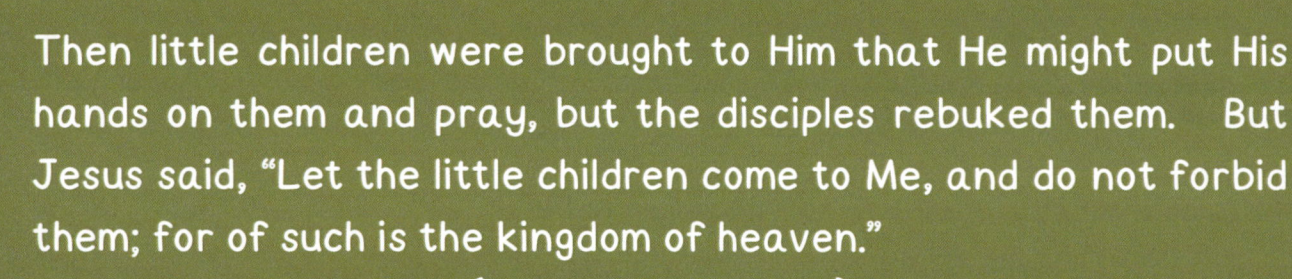

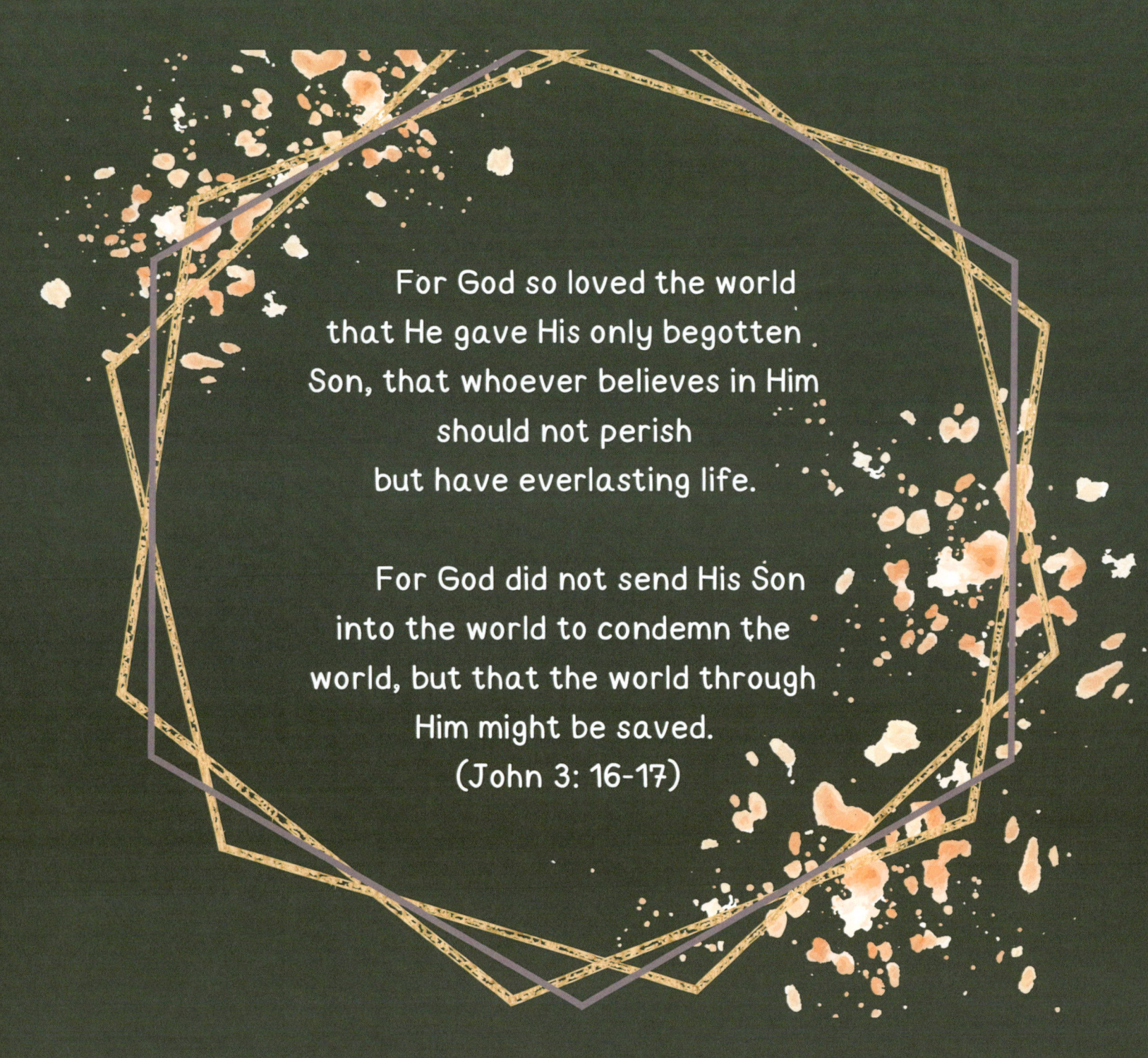

For God so loved the world that He gave His only begotten Son, that whoever believes in Him should not perish but have everlasting life.

For God did not send His Son into the world to condemn the world, but that the world through Him might be saved.
(John 3: 16-17)

Jesus, the Son of God, our Lord and Savior, Welcomes you...

Jesus loves me This... Big!

By Grace Alone, through Faith Alone, in Christ Alone.

Jesus loves me this I know
For the Bible tells me so.
Little ones to Him belong
They are weak, But He is strong.

Yes, Jesus loves me
Yes, Jesus loves me
Yes, Jesus loves me
The Bible tells me so.

Jesus loves me, He who died
Heaven's gate to open wide
He will wash away my sin,
Let His little child come in.

Yes, Jesus loves me
Yes, Jesus loves me
Yes, Jesus loves me
The Bible tells me so.

Amen

Merry Christmas

joyinthemidst.com

And so remember…

Seven hundred years prior to Jesus being born, His birth was predicted by Isaiah.

"For unto us a Child is born, unto us a Son is given; and the government will be upon His shoulder. And His name will be called Wonderful, Counselor, Mighty God, Everlasting Father, Prince of Peace."(Isaiah 9:6)

I love the presents, the food, the songs, the decorations, Christmas pageants and the candle lighting ceremonies. Yet, I grieve that for many people, the story ends with a baby. The amazing true story continues today with lives being changed by the power of Christ. By grace alone, through faith alone, in Christ alone. (From Ephesians 2:8)

This is my Christmas prayer and blessing for you, your children and grandchildren:

"For this reason, I bow my knees to the Father of our Lord Jesus Christ, from whom the whole family in heaven and earth is named, that He would grant you, according to the riches of His glory, to be strengthened with might through His Spirit in the inner man, that Christ may dwell in your hearts through faith; that you, being rooted and grounded in love, may be able to comprehend with all the saints what is the width and length and depth and height, to know the love of Christ which passes knowledge; that you may be filled with all the fullness of God." (Ephesians 3:14-20)

May "O Glorious Hope" be a tool for Christmas celebration and worship in your home for many years.

My Heart to Yours,

Anne M. Del Vecchio, Author Illustrator

Rejoice in the Lord always Again I say Rejoice.
Philippians 4:4

Family Record for This Book

First Purchased by _____ on _____

Passed Along With Love to _____on_____

Passed Along With Love to _____on_____

Passed Along With Love to _____on_____

Special Notes:

www.ingramcontent.com/pod-product-compliance
Lightning Source LLC
Chambersburg PA
CBRC100812010526
44107CB00023B/1274